Investigating Forces

Reader

Core Knowledge®

Copyright © 2019 Core Knowledge Foundation
www.coreknowledge.org

All Rights Reserved.

Core Knowledge®, Core Knowledge Curriculum Series™,
Core Knowledge Science™, and CKSci™ are trademarks
of the Core Knowledge Foundation.

Trademarks and trade names are shown in this book
strictly for illustrative and educational purposes and are
the property of their respective owners. References herein
should not be regarded as affecting the validity of said
trademarks and trade names.

Printed in Canada

ISBN: 978-1-68380-502-1

Investigating Forces

Table of Contents

Chapter 1	**A Force Is a Push or a Pull**	1
Chapter 2	**Friction Is a Force**	7
Chapter 3	**Predicting Patterns of Motion**	13
Chapter 4	**Magnetism Is a Force**	19
Chapter 5	**Solving Problems with Magnets**	25
Chapter 6	**Forces and Trains**	31
Glossary		37

A Force Is a Push or a Pull

Think about how you start your day. You wake up and push yourself out of bed. You pull a box from the shelf and pour cereal into a bowl. You lift a milk carton and pour the milk. Then, you pull spoonfuls of cereal to your mouth.

Big Question

What are balanced and unbalanced forces?

You might not wake up thinking that you are using forces, but you are. A **force** is a push or a pull. Each time you push or pull

Vocabulary

force, n. a push or a pull

something, you use a force. Every time something starts to move, stops moving, or changes direction, forces are involved.

What forces does the girl use to prepare and eat her breakfast?

1

Forces Change Motion

Whenever you cause something to start to move, stop moving, change speed, or change direction, you use forces.

Motion is a change of position. Think about kicking a ball. A force from your leg causes the ball to move—the ball is pushed into motion. The force of the kick changes the ball from not moving to moving. As the ball changes location, it is in motion.

Vocabulary

motion, n. the process of an object changing position

A bike rider pushes the bike's pedals to begin moving in a race. He pushes the handlebars to change directions to zigzag around the cones. The rider uses forces to change his direction and speed.

Forces can also make things stop moving. When the rider is ready to stop, he will stop pushing the bike pedals. He will pull on the bicycle brakes in a way that slows him down.

The rider uses forces to start, change, and stop his motion.

Forces Can Be Balanced or Unbalanced

When two equal teams play tug-of-war, the rope may not move at all. There is no motion. If you add up all the forces acting on the rope, they are equal. The pull from one side equals the pull from the other side. The forces on the rope are **balanced forces**.

The rope does not move when the two teams pull with equal force.

What happens to the rope when one side pulls with greater force than the other side? Forces on the rope become unbalanced. **Unbalanced forces** cause an object's motion to change. One team will begin to win the tug-of-war.

Imagine the tug-of-war rope sitting still on the ground. You might be surprised that forces are acting on it. The force of gravity is pulling the rope down all the time. The ground also pushes up against the rope. The two forces are equal but acting in opposite directions. How could you make the forces unbalanced and change the motion of the rope? By pulling on it to pick it up!

Vocabulary

balanced forces, n. a collection of forces acting on an object that cancel each other out and produce no change in the object's motion

unbalanced forces, n. a collection of forces acting on an object that result in a change in the object's motion

3

Gravity Is a Pulling Force

Forces are all around you. You can see or feel many of them, especially when they are unbalanced. You feel forces when someone pushes you on a swing. You feel a pull when someone tugs on your shirt.

You might not see or notice it, but the force of **gravity** pulls on you all the time. Earth's gravity is a force that pulls objects down toward the ground.

Vocabulary

gravity, n. a force that pulls objects toward Earth's surface

When you are sitting still, are forces acting on you? Yes! The force of the ground is pushing upward on your body, and the force of gravity is pulling you down. You don't float up or sink down because the forces are balanced. If you jump up, the push you apply with your muscles makes the forces unbalanced. You move upward.

Gravity pulls the boy downward. He pushes against the force with his legs as he balances.

A Force Has Direction

The dogs in the picture play tug with the rope toy. When the dogs pull the toy with the same amount of force, the toy does not move. The forces are balanced. The balanced forces have the same strength. But the forces pull in opposite directions.

One way to understand forces is to draw arrows to represent their direction. One dog pulls the rope toy to the left. The other dog pulls the toy to the right. Using arrows on pictures can help us model, or show, that all forces have direction.

The dogs pull the rope with the same amount of force but in different directions.

A Force Has Strength

Look at the picture. Which dog do you think will win the tugging match? The brown and white dog on the left is bigger. It can probably pull with a stronger force.

When two forces of different strengths pull on the same object, the object will move toward the stronger pull. When two forces of different strength push on an object, the object moves away from the stronger push. When pushes and pulls are balanced, the object will not move.

Can you predict if something will move when it is pushed or pulled? If you think carefully about strength and directions of all forces on an object, you can predict motion of the object. Try it yourself! You can draw pictures and arrows to help explain what causes something to move or stop moving.

These are unbalanced forces because one dog pulls with a stronger force.

Friction Is a Force

Have you ever tried to walk on ice? You probably know how easy it is to slip and fall. That's because there is little **friction** between your shoes and the ice. You don't slip when you walk on a rough sidewalk. There is a lot of friction between the sidewalk and your shoes.

Friction is the force that exists between two surfaces that are touching each other. Friction **opposes** motion or potential motion. When there is little friction, surfaces slide smoothly across each other. Friction reduces the slipping or even stops motion.

Big Question

What is the force called friction?

Vocabulary

friction, n. a force that occurs between the surfaces of two objects that are touching

oppose, v. to work against

This sign warns that there may be little friction between your shoes and the surface you are walking on. *Watch out!*

There is little friction between the bottom of the sled and the surface of the snow. The sled slides easily.

Surfaces in Contact Make Friction

Friction is a **contact force**. That means it happens where surfaces touch each other. For example, your shoes touch the sidewalk as you walk, and the force of friction helps you to propel yourself forward.

Vocabulary

contact force, n.
a push or pull between two objects that are touching each other

No object is completely smooth. Even things that look smooth have bumps too small to see or feel. When two objects rub against each other, those bumps push against each other.

Feet in socks slip and slide on a smooth floor.

Feet in socks do not slip against the rough material of carpet.

Some surfaces are very rough. Rough surfaces produce a lot of friction when in contact with other objects. Other surfaces are smooth. Smooth surfaces produce less friction when in contact with another surface.

Think about hurrying through different rooms wearing just socks and no shoes. You are less likely to slip on a carpeted surface than you are on a smooth floor.

Friction Opposes Motion and Potential Motion

Look at the picture of the block on the ramp. Are there forces at work there? Yes, there are. The force of gravity is pulling the block downward.

However, the block does not move. That is because there is a friction force between the block and the ramp. The friction opposes the force of gravity. When the two forces are balanced, there is no change in the block's motion. In this way, friction opposes the potential motion of the block.

Now, what would happen if you lift the ramp higher at one end? At some point, the force of gravity would overcome the force of friction. The forces would become unbalanced. Movement occurs as the block slides down the ramp.

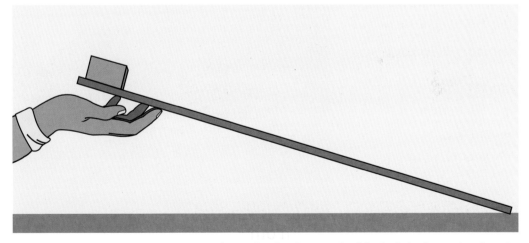

The block stays at rest on this piece of wood. Why doesn't the block slide down the slope?

Friction Produces Heat

Have you ever been outside in the cold and rubbed your hands together to try to warm them up? If so, you were making use of friction. Any time two surfaces rub against each other, heat may occur.

You can feel the heat produced by friction between your moving hands. The longer you rub them together and the harder you press them against each other, the warmer they will feel. If two surfaces only rub against each other briefly, the friction does not cause very much heat. Often the amount of heat produced is too little to notice. Do your socks feel warm after you slide across a tile floor?

Sometimes friction can result in a great deal of heat. It is possible to rub string and wood together in a way that the friction can start a fire.

To start a fire using only string and wood, the friction must continue steadily for a long while. The friction must also be concentrated in a small area.

Friction Can Be Harmful

It can be useful to know how to start a fire using friction. But heat from friction is not always helpful. Engines, such as the ones that make cars and planes move, have many moving parts. The parts are in contact with

The parts inside engines are coated with oil to reduce friction.

each other, so they are affected by the force of friction. The friction results in heat. Over time, friction and heat weaken the parts of machines. The parts can wear out and break.

Engineers use materials called **lubricants** to reduce friction between machine parts. A lubricant is a substance that coats the surfaces of parts that rub against each other to make them more slippery. Grease and oil are common lubricants. Lubricants help machine parts last longer.

Vocabulary

lubricant, n. a substance that reduces friction between objects in contact

Think About Water and Air

Friction affects more than just solid objects. Feeling the wind blowing on your face is evidence that moving air produces friction. Air friction is called air resistance or drag. Athletes such as professional bikers and swimmers wear special uniforms to reduce the amount of drag they experience as they race to the finish line.

Friction Can Be Helpful

Engineers don't always try to reduce friction. Often they design ways to make use of friction. For example, tires are designed with bumps and grooves on the surface that rolls on the road. Those bumps are called tread. Tread increases the friction between the surfaces of tires and the road. Without tread, a bicycle rider might slip and slide instead of rolling over a very smooth surface.

Squeezing a bicycle hand brake causes the brakes to press and rub against the bike wheel's rim. The force of friction that results makes the bike slow down or stop.

Don't touch a bicycle brake just after a bike has been stopped by the brake. It is likely hot from the friction.

Predicting Patterns of Motion

Forces can get things moving. A force can also change the speed or direction of an object's motion. When regular forces help move an object up and down, side to side, back and forth, or in a zigzag motion, you may be able to notice a regular pattern of motion as a result.

Big Question

Can we predict the motion of an object that moves in regular patterns?

A child swings back and forth at a playground. Once the force of her muscles gets her going, she stops applying muscle force, and her motion becomes regular. She goes forward and backward. She goes up and then down. As she swings, only the forces of gravity and friction affect her motion.

What forces act to get the girl moving, and what forces act on her as she swings?

Patterns of Motion

Back and Forth

Look! At the highest part of her swing, the girl is at rest for just a moment. While she is still, at that highest point, only one force, gravity, is acting on her. The force of gravity has slowed her down, and now her motion has stopped. What happens next? The force of Earth's gravity continues to pull her toward the ground. Then she will move backward and swing to another high point on the other side. She will come to a rest again.

You could record data of her movements in a science notebook. You could use this data to show that all her motion repeats in a pattern if the same pushes and pulls continue.

Other forces will also affect her motion as she swings. Air brushes across her. The hinges on the swing rub against the chain of the swing. If the girl does not use her muscles to keep swinging, friction will slow her down and eventually cause her to stop.

Up and Down

To **predict** is to say something that is expected to happen. Knowing about an object's pattern of motion helps you predict how it will move next.

Vocabulary

predict, v. to say that something is expected to happen

Look at the two friends in this picture. They are playing on a seesaw. One girl used the force of her leg muscles to push herself up. This force is now greater than the force of gravity on the girl. She goes up. When she does, the other girl moves down.

In a moment, the lower girl will push herself up with the force of the muscles in her legs. It is easy to predict how she will move and how the other girl will move because these movements are part of a regular pattern.

Based on what you know about the movement of a seesaw, can you predict what will happen next? Can you identify the forces that change the seesaw's motion?

Back and Forth

The movement of this clock's hands are caused by the regular pattern of the clock's pendulum.

The part hanging below the face of this clock is a pendulum. A pendulum is a device in which a weight, called a bob, swings back and forth. Each swing takes the same amount of time. Back and forth it swings. The motion is regular. That means it is a **pattern** that repeats itself over and over.

What is the pendulum's pattern of motion, and how can you predict future motion?

The pendulum swings back and forth, much like the girl on the playground's swing. A pendulum experiences the same forces, gravity and friction, as it moves.

Vocabulary

pattern, n. something that keeps repeating

Patterns exist everywhere, from shapes to relationships to seasons.

Patterns of Motion Are Predictable

Hardly anything is more predicable than the movement of the hands of a clock. The pendulum swings, and time ticks on. The hands move from 1:00, to 1:15, to 1:30, and so on.

Clocks are designed to display the time based on regular patterns of motion. It is easy to predict motion in the future if you can describe and understand its regular patterns.

A clock like this displays several patterns of motion. The pendulum swings back and forth. Left, center, right, back to center, left, and so on. The minute hand rotates. It points to all the numbers around the circular clock face once every hour. The hour hand rotates. It points to all the numbers around the circular clock face once every twelve hours.

Around and Around

This boy and girl are playing tetherball. They are using the muscles in their arms to move the ball. The goal of the game is to wrap the rope around the pole.

The girl has made the ball go around the pole three times. Predict what the ball will do when she pushes it again. If her opponent never hits the ball, the ball will go around and around in the same direction of the push given to it by the girl. It's easy to predict possible motion once you understand a regular pattern.

Think of things that move up and down, around in circles, and back and forth. When you observe regular patterns in an object's motion, you can predict which way it will move next.

What is the tetherball's pattern of motion if the boy never hits the ball?

Magnetism Is a Force

You place a **magnet** on a refrigerator door, and it sticks there. Why? It sticks because of a force called **magnetism**.

You hold a magnet over a pile of iron paper clips, and the clips move toward the magnet. Magnetism is the invisible force that pulls on some metal objects.

Big Question

What are the characteristics of the force called magnetism?

Vocabulary

magnet, n. a material that applies the force of magnetism

magnetism, n. a force that can push or pull on some materials without touching them

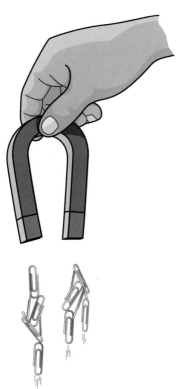

Most forces exist between objects that are touching each other. Magnetism is different, though. Magnetism acts across a distance. Objects that are affected by magnets do not have to be touching the magnets.

Magnets Attract Many Kinds of Metal Objects

People first learned about magnetism from a rock called lodestone. Lodestone has a lot of iron in it. Magnetism happens naturally in lodestone, but natural magnets are rare.

People can turn some metals into magnets, though. This process is called *magnetizing* an object. Magnets are most often made of iron, but other types of metal can be magnetized, too. A metal that has been magnetized is called *magnetic*.

Magnets contain metal, and they often affect other metal objects. That is true even if those other metal objects are not magnetic themselves. Your refrigerator door is not magnetic, but you can hang pictures on it using a magnet. Magnets do not affect objects that aren't metal. Wood, water, and plastic are examples of things not attracted by magnets.

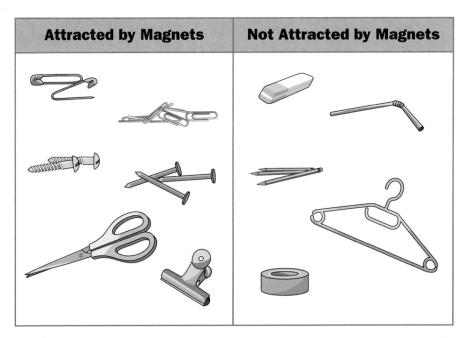

Attracted by Magnets	Not Attracted by Magnets

The force of magnetism does not affect objects that do not contain any metal.

Magnetism Is a Force That Can Push and Pull

Two magnets affect each other in predictable ways. Sometimes they push each other. The pushing force makes them move farther apart. When two magnets are pushing each other apart, you can push harder to move the magnets together. The force of your pushing can overcome the force of the two magnets.

Other times, magnets pull each other. The pulling force makes them move closer together. Magnets that pull each other will usually move closer together until they touch. Very strong magnets can be hard to pull apart.

Both magnetic pulls and magnetic pushes happen across a distance. If you put a thin piece of paper between two magnets that are pulling on each other, they will continue to pull each other.

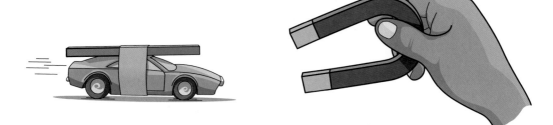

In this picture the toy car has a magnet taped to its top. The magnet is being pulled by the other magnet. Which direction do you think the toy car will move?

Every Magnet Has Two Poles

A magnet has **magnetic poles**. One pole is called the *north pole*. The other pole is called the *south pole*. Every magnet has two opposite poles.

When the north poles of two different magnets face each other, the magnets **repel**. When magnets repel each other, it means that they push each other away. When the same poles of two different magnets are near each other, they will repel. The south poles of two magnets repel each other, too.

Vocabulary

magnetic poles, n. the places on a magnet where the magnetic force is strongest

repel, v. to push away from

attract, v. to pull something closer

When the north pole of one magnet faces the south pole of another magnet, the magnets **attract**. Two magnets attract each other when they pull toward each other. When the opposite poles of two magnets are near each other, they will attract.

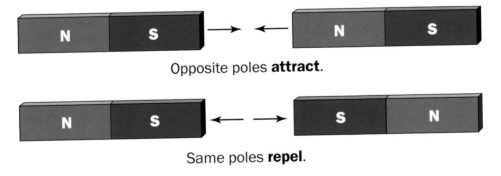

Opposite poles **attract**.

Same poles **repel**.

North and south poles attract. When south and south poles are near each other, they repel each other. When north and north poles are near each other, they repel each other.

Strength of Magnetism Changes with Distance

A magnet does not have to touch an object to attract it. At the same time, a magnet that is too far from a metal object will not affect it at all. The closer a magnet is to some metals, the stronger its attraction.

Magnetism also affects some metals more strongly than others. Iron is a metal that is strongly affected by magnetism. The metal nickel, but not the coin, also responds to magnetism. Nickel is one of the metals used to make a lot of magnets. Cans that food comes in are mostly made of steel. These cans can be picked up using a magnet because steel is made mostly of iron.

Many metals are not affected by magnets. The metal aluminum does not respond to magnetism. Cans made of aluminum cannot be picked up using a magnet. Many refrigerators are made with stainless steel. Stainless steel is not attracted to magnets. Some companies use regular steel behind the stainless steel so magnets can stick to the refrigerator.

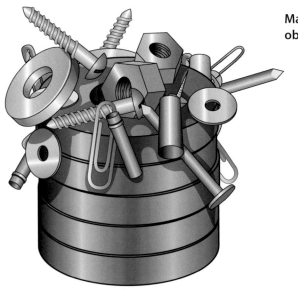

Magnetic force can pull on some metal objects through other metal objects.

Magnetism Can Be Useful

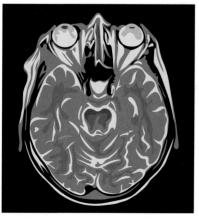

Computers and **household electronics** use magnets to store data in computer memory. Electronic speakers also use magnets to produce sounds you hear, including from a cell phone and computer speakers.

Medical machines use magnets to see inside the body. A computer receives the signals that show changes in magnetism. The machine converts those signals to pictures of what is inside the human body. This MRI picture shows the inside of a person's head.

Compasses use magnets to show direction. The needle of the compass is magnetic and is affected by the Earth's magnetic field.

Jewelry clasps are small and hard to hook together. By using the attraction of magnets, a magnetic clasp is easy to put together. You just put the ends of a magnetic jewelry clasp near each other, and they pull together.

Solving Problems with Magnets

People make notes to remind themselves of important things. One **problem** is that it can be easy to forget about a reminder note. The note has to be in a place where you are likely to see it.

Engineers know that people have problems, wants, and needs. For example, you might want a way to hang notes where you are likely to see them. And perhaps you want to do this without using sticky tape or tacks that would damage your walls. Magnets provide a **solution** for the problem. A magnet sticks to a refrigerator. It can hold a note where people are likely to see it. But the magnet is easy to remove without leaving any permanent marks.

A refrigerator magnet is a solution designed to solve a problem. It's a simple solution, but it works!

Big Question

What problems can be solved with magnets?

Vocabulary

problem, n. a want or need that requires a solution

solution, n. a plan or object that solves a problem

A solution meets a want or need.

If the silver disk is a magnet, what kind of material is the refrigerator made of?

Magnets Help Find Where a Picture Hook Should Go

Suppose you have a room with a big, empty wall. It needs some decoration. You decide you want to hang a picture. The picture is heavy.

When you look at the orange wall, you cannot tell where the studs are.

Walls in most homes are hollow with frames inside them. The frames are made of boards called studs. Often the studs are made of wood. The smooth wall material that you see in a room is not strong enough to hold a heavy picture or a TV. If you want to hang something heavy on a wall, you must put a nail or screw into one of the wooden studs that you can't see.

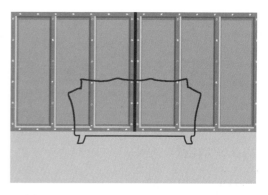

Hidden inside the wall are studs that contain metal screws or nails.

Though the studs are made of wood, they contain many hidden nails and screws. Nails and screws are made of metal.

How can you find a wooden wall stud? That is a problem. Engineers design solutions to problems. Engineers solved this problem by designing stud finders. A stud finder has a magnet inside. The magnet is attracted to metal nails in the studs behind the solid wall. It detects where nails are. This reveals where the studs are and where you can securely place a picture hook. Engineers used magnetism to design and build stud finders—and they really work.

Engineers use the properties of a magnet to solve the problem of finding where a nail in a stud is behind a wall.

Magnets Are Important for Modern Railroads

Ordinary trains have metal wheels that run on metal tracks. The friction between the track and the wheels is necessary for movement. But it also wears out the train's moving parts.

Most modern passenger trains have metal wheels that roll on metal tracks. Too much friction between the wheels and the track is a problem.

The need to make a train that works with less friction is an engineering problem.

Engineers designed and developed trains that use magnets for motion. What a solution! The magnetic trains are called *maglevs*. Maglevs use magnetism so the train floats above the track without metal wheels. That means less friction.

A maglev train works without wheels touching tracks. That's a solution.

Engineers Design Solutions Before They Build

About eight hundred years ago, Petrus Peregrinus de Maricourt invented the first compasses. He knew magnets pointed to the north and south. He also knew a needle could be made magnetic. It would then point to the north and south. All that was left to do was design a way for the needle to float. He used his knowledge of magnets and magnetic poles to suggest a way to find direction.

He first designed a solution to a problem. Perhaps he made a model first. Perhaps he drew it out on paper. After he made his engineering design, he could proceed to build a compass.

Petrus Peregrinus de Maricourt was a French scholar. He figured out how to use magnets to find directions.

A modern compass is lightweight and easy to carry in a pocket.

Engineers work on solutions to problems. They often work in teams.

When engineers look for a solution to a problem, they first design what they want. They also think about these challenges:

- **Time:** How long will it take to solve the problem? Is that time used worth the result?

- **Cost:** How much will it cost to solve the problem? Will the solution cost more money than it saves? Can it be done with the amount of money available?

- **Materials:** What materials are needed to solve the problem? Is it easy to get the tools needed?

- **Limits:** What are some things I can't do or am not allowed to do?

Even eight hundred years ago de Maricourt asked these questions. In fact, as long as people need to solve problems, their design process will involve thinking about time, cost, material, and limits to come up with a good solution.

Forces and Trains

Elijah McCoy was born in Canada. His parents had been slaves in Kentucky. They escaped to freedom on the Underground Railroad before Elijah was born.

Big Question

How have engineering designers improved trains?

The family moved to Michigan. That state did not have slavery. Elijah got training as a mechanical engineer. But he could not get a good job. Most places at that time would not hire African Americans for jobs that paid well.

He found low-paying work at a railroad company. There, even though improving trains was not his job, he found solutions to problems anyway. His inventions helped shape the Industrial Revolution.

Elijah McCoy was an engineer and inventor who lived from 1844 to 1929.

Words to Know

Some slaves used the *Underground Railroad* to escape to freedom. It was not a real railroad. It was a system of roads and hiding places.

The *Industrial Revolution* was a period of rapidly developing technology growth that occurred in the 1800s.

A Strong Force Is Needed to Move a Train at Rest

A long train needs a powerful force to get moving.

Before trains, people transported materials by foot, by animals, or by boat. Trains made it possible to move large amounts of things that people needed across great distances.

Trains are made of heavy metal. They carry people and cargo. They carry fuel for the train to move. All this makes trains very heavy.

Words to Know

To *overcome* means to get past an obstacle. Overcoming a force requires the use of a different, stronger force.

A train at rest is hard to move. When trains are at rest, forces are balanced. The train must create an unbalanced force to start to move.

Engineers like Elijah McCoy studied the problem of making a train move. They developed many different solutions to the problem of *overcoming* the forces of gravity and friction.

Making Trains Move Requires Engineering Solutions

This is a picture of an early train made from heavy metal. The locomotive burned coal or wood to heat a tank of water. The water became steam. The motion energy of moving steam turned the parts that powered the wheels.

Starting a train moving takes force. But keeping it moving also takes force to overcome friction and gravity.

One way to solve the problem of getting a train to start moving is to make it out of lighter metals. A train made from such metals needs less force to set it into motion.

Starting a train moving is one problem. There are other problems in building working trains. Friction and heat cause engines to wear out. Engineers have to design wheels that have just enough, but not too much, friction with the tracks.

Lubrication is a solution for friction. But in McCoy's day lubricating engines had a problem. To be lubricated, the train had to be stopped. That slowed down service. It also meant that more fuel was needed to make the train move again. The process was expensive.

McCoy's automatic lubricator worked as the train was moving. It saved railroads time and money.

Lubricating train engines was part of Elijah McCoy's job. He invented a way to do it without stopping the train. Then he found ways to make his invention even better. He also invented other solutions that solved many other train problems. He used the principles of engineering design to make sure his invention would work.

Whenever he made something new, he got a patent for it. A patent is a certificate from the government. It gives an inventor credit for an invention. Only the inventor can make money from a patented invention. Elijah ended up with sixty patents for the engineering designs and things he invented.

Words to Know

A *patent* is a government document that gives someone the ownership and rights to an invention. Thousands of new patents for engineering design solutions were filed during the Industrial Revolution.

Modern Trains

A magnetic train, or maglev

Mr. McCoy was an engineering designer and an engineer too. People in his profession have continued to make trains better. They develop trains that weigh less. By studying forces and motion, they learn to get trains to start and move faster. Modern trains also meet strict standards for pollution control.

Engineers have improved on McCoy's efforts. They have developed magnetic trains, or maglevs. Maglevs don't use wheels and tracks like regular trains do. They use magnets. The force of magnetism can cause an entire train to be lifted above the track and be moved forward. That removes almost all the friction because the train and tracks never come into contact. Removing friction makes train rides quiet and smooth.

How Maglevs Work

The word *maglev* is short for magnetic levitation. *Levitation* means floating in the air.

Maglevs levitate. Maglevs are designed with magnets in both the trains and the track. The force of magnets' same poles pushes the train up off of the track. The push between the magnets is stronger than the force of gravity pulling the train down. So, the train seems to float above the track. And since no surfaces are touching, there is no friction. This allows maglev trains to move very fast.

Words to Know

To *levitate* means to float in the air.

The word part *levi-* comes from the Latin word *levis*, meaning "light."

Maglev magnets are electrical. They can be turned on and off. Their poles can be switched. Their strength can also be controlled. Computers control the magnets so that their repelling forces move the train along the track without touching it.

Train engineers have followed in the footsteps of Elijah McCoy. Engineers are always improving maglev technology to improve how the trains work. More and better maglevs are appearing in countries all over the world.

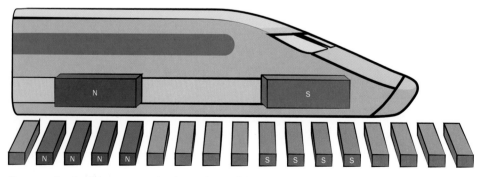

Same poles in the magnets in the train and the track keep the two from touching.

Glossary

A

attract, v. to pull something closer **(22)**

B

balanced forces, n. a collection of forces acting on an object that cancel each other out and produce no change in the object's motion **(3)**

C

contact force, n. a push or pull between two objects that are touching each other **(8)**

F

force, n. a push or a pull **(1)**

friction, n. a force that occurs between the surfaces of two objects that are touching **(7)**

G

gravity, n. a force that pulls objects toward Earth's surface **(4)**

L

lubricant, n. a substance that reduces friction between objects in contact **(11)**

M

magnet, n. a material that applies the force of magnetism **(19)**

magnetic poles, n. the places on a magnet where the magnetic force is strongest **(22)**

magnetism, n. a force that can push or pull on some materials without touching them **(19)**

motion, n. the process of an object changing position **(2)**

O

oppose, v. to work against **(7)**

P

pattern, n. something that keeps repeating **(16)**

predict, v. to say that something is expected to happen **(15)**

problem, n. a want or need that requires a solution **(25)**

R

repel, v. to push away from **(22)**

S

solution, n. a plan or object that solves a problem **(25)**

U

unbalanced forces, n. a collection of forces acting on an object that result in a change in the object's motion **(3)**

Core Knowledge®

CKSci™
Core Knowledge SCIENCE™

Editorial Directors
Daniel H. Franck and Richard B. Talbot

Subject Matter Expert

Martin Rosenberg, PhD
Teacher of Physics and Computer Science
SAR High School
Riverdale, New York

Illustrations and Photo Credits

Agencja Fotograficzna Caro / Alamy Stock Photo: 5

Anthony Collins Cycling / Alamy Stock Photo: 12

Barrie Harwood / Alamy Stock Photo: 33

Bernd Mellmann / Alamy Stock Photo: i, iii, 35

Bildarchiv Monheim GmbH / Alamy Stock Photo: 34

Bill Grant / Alamy Stock Photo: 15

Don Smetzer / Alamy Stock Photo: 32

EyeEm / Alamy Stock Photo: 8b

GOODLUZ / Alamy Stock Photo: 30

Hero Images Inc. / Alamy Stock Photo: 27

Hero Images / SuperStock: 10

Jimj0will / Alamy Stock Photo: 6

Kuttig - People - 2 / Alamy Stock Photo: 7b

Lumi Images / Alamy Stock Photo: 13

Malcolm Fairman / Alamy Stock Photo: 28a

Maskot / SuperStock: 25

Mike Kemp / Blend Images / SuperStock: 1

OpenClipart-Vectors / Pixabay: 7a

Paul Doyle / Alamy Stock Photo: 4

Phil Crean A / Alamy Stock Photo: 29b

Pictorial Press Ltd / Alamy Stock Photo: 31

Robertharding / SuperStock: 28b

Roman Kosolapov / Alamy Stock Photo: 8a

RosalreneBetancourt 6 / Alamy Stock Photo: 2

Stephen Dorey ABIPP / Alamy Stock Photo: 11

View Stock / Alamy Stock Photo: Cover D, 3

World History Archive / SuperStock: 29